PUFFIN BOOKS

ON THE NIGHT WATCH

It's no wonder that Miss Finstock looks worried after the phone call from the council. They've decided not to spend any more money on the school – no more paint, or dinners, or lights – in fact there's to be no more school. The pupils are all very upset and worried, but their parents are angry and they decide to work out a plan to *make* the council listen to their views. Soon the whole town is up in arms.

Hannah Cole was born in London and spent the first twenty years of her life living in Hammersmith. She now lives in Oxford, where she works in a day centre for mentally handicapped adults.

Hannah Cole

On the Night Watch

Illustrated by Kate Rogers

PUFFIN BOOKS

Puffin Books, Penguin Books Ltd, Harmondsworth, Middlesex, England
Viking Penguin Inc., 40 West 23rd Street, New York, New York 10010, U.S.A.
Penguin Books Australia Ltd, Ringwood, Victoria, Australia
Penguin Books Canada Limited, 2801 John Street, Markham, Ontario, Canada L3R 1B4
Penguin Books (N.Z.) Ltd, 182–190 Wairau Road, Auckland 10, New Zealand

First published by Julia MacRae Books 1984
Published in Puffin Books 1987

Copyright © Hannah Cole, 1984
Illustrations copyright © Kate Rogers, 1984
All rights reserved

Printed and bound in Great Britain by
Cox & Wyman Ltd, Reading

Except in the United States of America, this book is sold subject
to the condition that it shall not, by way of trade or otherwise, be lent,
re-sold, hired out, or otherwise circulated without the
publisher's prior consent in any form of binding or cover other than
that in which it is published and without a similar condition
including this condition being imposed on the subsequent purchaser

Contents

1 A Phone Call – Bad News, 9

2 The Last Day and the First Night, 20

3 The Banner for the Rooftop, 31

4 A Knock in the Night, 41

5 Marching into Town, 51

For Marianne

1 A Phone Call – Bad News

There was no yellow. Mrs. Cowley had done her very best with the rest of the paints. She had mixed up purple and grey, pink and three kinds of blue, bright red and dark red as well as black and white. Zafar was painting a really good picture of a football match; you hardly noticed that the grass was blue instead of green. And Tracey's cars looked fine. She was painting the cars that her dad made every day at the factory.

"I do like these colours," said Janet. "They would be nice for a pattern. But they aren't the colours I need for my picture."

"Oh dear," said Mrs. Cowley. "It is a bit tricky, isn't it, without any yellow. What are

you trying to paint, my duck?"

"I'm painting a jungle," said Janet. "I need yellow for the tiger's stripes, and for the bananas on the trees. I need orange for the lion and the giraffe and the sun. And I need green for all the rest of the jungle. You haven't mixed any green."

"I'm afraid I can't mix green without using yellow," said Mrs. Cowley. "How about painting a magic jungle, where everything is bewitched into a different colour? Purple tigers and blue bananas."

Janet looked at the purple paint brush and wondered if it would paint a magic tiger for her.

"That would be a good picture if I could get the shapes right," she said. "But with the colours wrong and the shapes a bit funny, nobody would ever guess what the picture was meant to be."

The phone started to ring and Janet saw Miss Finstock go to answer it. When she came back, she spoke to Mrs. Cowley. They both looked worried and angry.

"I bet that phone call was the paint suppliers," said Zafar. "Saying they still won't bring any yellow paint. Look how cross they both are."

"Time to clear up now," Miss Finstock called out. "Put all the paint brushes in the sink. Careful, Tracey. Oh, Tracey! Now you will have to get the cloth. Hurry up, now, children. Don't forget to wash your hands."

Janet had hardly started to paint, so she was the first to be cleared up.

"When will the paint suppliers send the

yellow, miss?" she asked.

"I don't think they will be sending it after all," said Miss Finstock, and her voice was wobbly. She was upset. "The Council don't want to spend any more money on this school."

"We'll have to give up painting when the red and blue run out," said Zafar.

"We'll have to give up eating too," said Vernon. "They won't pay for our dinners either, I don't suppose."

"The Council just telephoned," said Miss Finstock. "I'm sorry to say that they don't want to spend any more money on paint, or dinners, or electric lights, or Mrs. Cowley's wages, or anything. They are going to close the school."

"Will we go to another school?" asked Janet.

"Of course, dear," said Miss Finstock. "Children who live to the west of Harwell Road will move to West Oxford First School, and children who live to the east will go to College Road School."

"You mean I'll have to go to a different school from Janet and Zafar?" said Vernon. "We've always been together."

"They are both nice schools," said Miss Finstock.

"They may be nice," said Patrick, "but they are miles away. My mum won't like walking all the way to West Oxford every morning, but it's too far for us to go by ourselves, with the main road. And our Bernie's only been at this school one term. She has only just got used to being here."

"My dad says this school is good because the classes are not too big," said Tracey. "If I go to College Road, I'll be in a much bigger class. I bet the teacher won't hear me reading every day."

"Now then," said Miss Finstock. "I don't want you to worry yourselves too much about it. I'll have a word with all your parents and explain what the Council has told me. You know, we've been very lucky to have this lovely school up till now, haven't we?"

"We won't be very lucky if they shut it up," said Zafar, "when we've just got it the way we like it. The big kids have only just finished those pictures on the playground wall, and all the parents came in last holidays to do up the hall. The Council can't stop us coming here."

"It's the Council who run the school," said Miss Finstock, "and if the Council decide to close it down, I don't know what we can do. But don't you bother your heads about it. Just let the grown-ups do the worrying. Now it's nearly time to go home, so put your chairs up and we'll get the place tidy."

It was sad to think of the summer coming, and nobody allowed to play in the sunny school garden with the climbing frame and the grassy

slopes. It was sad to think of the empty classroom, with the paints and glue and books tidily put away on the shelves, never being used.

Mothers and fathers and minders had already started to arrive in the playground. Janet's dad always came for her because they lived the other side of the main road. Today he looked angry. He had heard the news about the Council. He was too angry to feel like cooking when they got back to the flat, so Janet made her own tea.

"Will I go to school in the morning?" she

asked as she wiped the last crumbs off the table. "Or have they shut it up already?"

"Tomorrow is the last day of term," said her dad. "They mean to lock it up tomorrow night. But we're not going to let them."

"That's good," said Janet. "I've been thinking. I don't always feel like going to school, but I would miss Mrs. Cowley and the guinea pig. I certainly don't feel like going to a strange school and getting used to it all over again. How are we going to stop them shutting it?"

Janet's dad put a crust out on the window-sill for the birds.

"I'm not sure yet," he said. "Tonight we're going to Tracey's house to meet all the others and work out a plan."

"Will all the children be there?" asked Janet.

"I expect most of them will be in bed. But all the parents will be there, and the teachers. You'll have to put on lots of clothes when we go, because even in this warm weather it gets cold out at night."

When it was time to go, Janet put on two jumpers and her winter coat. Her dad lent her his red scarf. It was very cold on the back of

his bike, where Janet sat. There was a wind blowing and Janet held on tight to the bottom of her dad's jacket. She leant her head back and looked up at the stars. Bits of the darkness got into her eyes. Her dad was excited and kept ringing the bicycle bell.

Tracey's front room was full of people. Zafar's mother had brought the baby, and it was asleep in its carry-cot under the table. All the

grown-ups talked and talked, and Janet fell asleep on her dad's lap. In the middle of the night, her dad carried her out and lifted her into the seat on the back of the bike. Janet leant against her dad's back, but it was a hard pillow, and kept moving from side to side as he pedalled. It was beautiful to get into her own comfortable bed at last.

2 The Last Day and the First Night

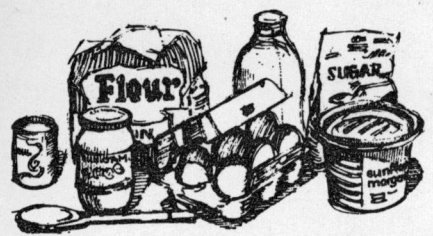

In the morning, school seemed the same as usual. Janet finished the work she had started the day before, and Zafar and Tracey pinned the class project up on the wall. When Miss Finstock let them choose, Janet and Vernon played in the wendy house. It was what they had liked best when they first started school, and now they might never have another chance.

"The little ones have let this house get in a terrible mess," said Janet. She sorted it out while Vernon cooked wonderful cakes out of lego bricks.

After the children's real dinner there was real cooking to be done. Mrs. Cowley helped them to make buns with jam in the middle. They

usually made enough for just one each, and that was all. Today Mrs. Cowley had lots of eggs and two whole packets of flour. They baked hundreds of buns.

"It's a pity I ate so much dinner," said Vernon. "I won't be able to eat many of these."

"They're not all for us, my love," said Mrs. Cowley. "There's other people will be wanting some too." But she did not say who. Janet began to guess who the buns were for when she looked out of the window at the end of the afternoon. The playground was much more crowded than usual.

The mothers and fathers and minders had brought some little brothers and sisters and a few babies, which was usual. But they had also brought some big brothers and sisters and an uncle or two. Even the biggest children's parents had come, and Tracey's mum, who lived right next to the school and did not need to fetch Tracey home. Tracey's mum walked straight into the classroom. Parents often came in to talk to Miss Finstock or to look for lost jumpers, but Tracey's mum was not looking for Tracey's jumper. She had a screwdriver, and she started to take the lock off the door.

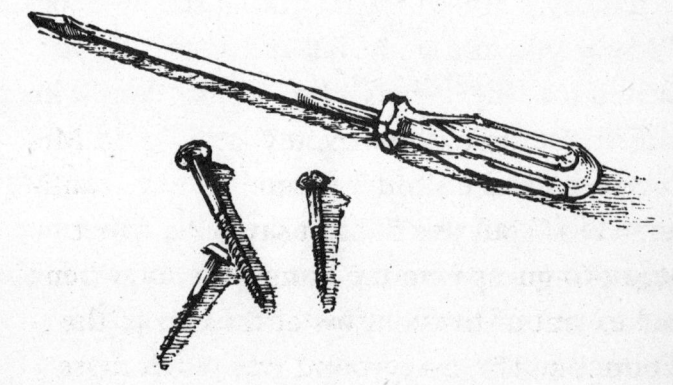

"What do you think you are doing?" asked Janet. "Whatever will Miss Finstock say?"

"It's all right, Janet," said Miss Finstock. "Tracey's mother will put a different lock on the door. Then when the Council man comes to lock the school up, his key won't fit. We shall have the key to fit the new lock, so we can lock the Council out. I must say, I wish it was not necessary, but I'm afraid they have left us no time to persuade them sensibly."

"Changing the lock is a very sensible way to persuade them," said Janet. "We can be looking after the school, and using it, while they are changing their minds."

Tracey's mum finished fixing the new lock. "I hear you and your dad are on the night watch tonight," she said to Janet. "You'll keep the Council out, won't you?"

Janet went to find her dad.

"What's all this?" she asked. "Is this what you grown-ups were planning last night, for me to be on the night watch and keep the Council out?"

"Someone has to stay here all the time to

keep guard," said her dad. "Because if they once lock us out, we'll have lost the school. So everyone will take turns. It's our turn tonight, with some other people."

"But all night!" said Janet. "Suppose they come down the chimney, or through the cloakroom window that doesn't shut? And suppose there are a lot of them? And supposing it gets cold at night, and we don't have anything to eat here except Miss Finstock's biscuits?"

"Look," said her dad. "We think it's important to keep the school open, don't we? So, we'll stay here to make sure they don't shut it. We'll have plenty to eat, and plenty of blankets to keep us warm. It will be fun. You'll see."

"Dad," said Janet. "You know I never can sleep without my rat. Don't you remember the time you washed her and she was too wet to go to bed with me?"

"You do worry, Jan," said her dad. "What do you suppose is in this great bag here?"

Janet looked in the bag. It had everything they might need – toothbrushes, a towel, Janet's special cream for behind her knees, a book for her dad to read, and Janet's toy rat.

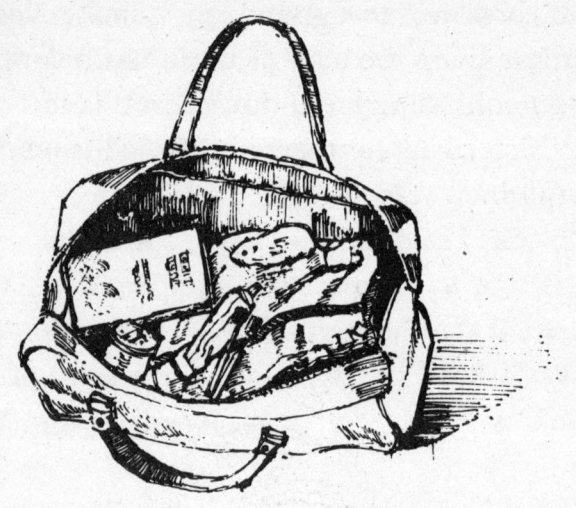

Janet took the rat into the wendy house, and put her toothbrush in the little cupboard. Zafar came and looked through the window.

"You are lucky," he said. "It's like camping. My brothers go camping with the Scouts. I've got to sleep at home tonight. But I'll be back in the morning. My mother is bringing breakfast for the guards."

"That's us," said Janet. "We're on the night watch. Will it be an Indian breakfast?"

"Yes," said Zafar. "Cornflakes and bread and butter, but maybe some English eggs."

Mrs. Cowley was giving jam buns to all the children, even the ones that did not belong to the school. There were just enough. Zafar's baby sister had a bun and squashed it on the floor, which was a waste.

The grown-ups were getting the school organised. Tracey's mum pushed the piano up against the cloakroom window, so that no-one could get in through it. Janet's dad was cleaning up the dusty spare classroom which was never used. "We can have more classes now," he said. "You will be less crowded, and Tracey's twins can come to school. They thought they would have to wait another term."

Patrick's dad moved the furniture in the hall so that there would be room for people to sleep there at night.

Vernon's father brought a huge pan of stew

and they heated it up on the stove. Janet and Vernon ate theirs in the wendy house, off the dolls' dishes. The wendy house sink had no real water. They licked the plates clean, and then they asked one of Zafar's big sisters to read them a story. She was too big for the wendy house, so she sat just outside and read to them through the window.

When Zafar and Vernon had gone home, Janet's dad said it was time for bed. "I'll be sleeping just outside your front door," he said, "so I won't be far away."

Janet only just fitted into the wendy house bed. The wendy house had no roof, so the

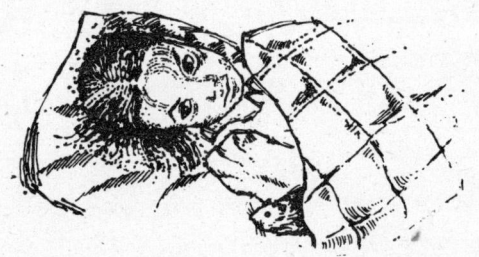

classroom ceiling was like the sky. It had cracks in it, but no stars. Janet could hear some grown-ups talking, and a typewriter was banging away. Vernon's father was smoking cigarettes. They smelt horrible.

Sometimes there was a knock on the door and Janet's dad would open it just a crack to see who it was. Each time it turned out to be someone coming to help guard the school. The Council never came at all.

The typewriter seemed to go on banging

away all night. But in Janet's dream the bang bang bang of the typewriter turned into nails that Tracey's mother was banging into the door, so that it was shut fast and safe against the Council.

3 The Banner for the Rooftop

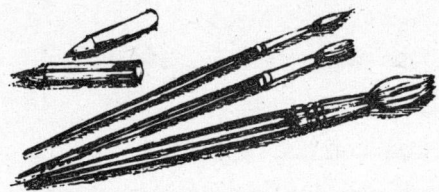

Janet woke because there was a clinking noise in the playground. It was nearly daylight. She drew the wendy house curtains and looked out into the classroom. Her dad was asleep on the floor with a blanket wrapped round him and his jumper bundled up under his head for a pillow. There were grown-ups asleep all over the floor on mattresses or in sleeping bags.

The milkman was outside clinking bottles. When Janet looked carefully, she saw that it was not a milkman but a milkwoman. In fact, it was Cathy who lived in their block of flats. The school was not really on her milk round, but she had come specially in case they needed extra milk. She had to hurry off to finish her

round. Janet heard the milk-float buzzing and clinking away down the road.

The grown-ups began to wake up and climb out of their sleeping bags. Janet's dad unwound his blanket and put his jumper on. Zafar's mother had arrived with the breakfast. Janet came out of the wendy house and ate her cornflakes with her dad at one of the desks. Her dad had to sit sideways because his long legs would not fit under the desk.

"You had better pack up your things," he told Janet. "The other children will be arriving soon, and the little ones may want to play in the wendy house."

Tracey's twins came. You had to remember that Duncan was the one with the sticking plaster on his knee. Also Robert cried more than Duncan, but sometimes Duncan cried too, so it was not a sure way of telling them apart.

Miss Finstock found places for the new children to put their coats. She made labels for their pegs, with pictures as well as names on, in

case the new children could not read.

"We can have two smaller classes now," said Miss Finstock. "The bigger children are coming in the new classroom with me, and the little ones will stay in here with Mrs. Cowley and Mr. Roger. Mr. Roger is a teacher who has no school to teach in at the moment, so he has come to help us."

Mr. Roger was rolling up his sleeves, as though he expected to do something very messy with the little children.

"I'm sharing out the books and equipment," said Mrs. Cowley. "So there will be some for each classroom."

"Will we have half the guinea pig each?" asked Zafar.

"Don't be silly," said Miss Finstock. "There are lots of things that we will share, like the musical instruments and the painting equipment. The two classes will do a lot of things together. We are sorting you out so that you know where you belong, and where your own boxes are. I will tell you whether you are big or little, and then the big ones can bring their boxes and come into the new classroom."

"I know I'm big," said Vernon.
"You're huge," said Zafar.
"I'm big," said Duncan, and Robert started to cry.
"No, you're not," said Tracey. "You're my

little twins, and you had better stay with Mrs. Cowley, because she knows how to look after babies."

Duncan began crying as well. Miss Finstock read out a list of all the children who were big enough to go with her. The twins were so small that she thought she could fit them into her classroom until they were used to being at school.

"Quickly, children," she said. "Find your boxes and come with me."

There was plenty of space in the new classroom. When the grown-ups had brought in some desks and cupboards, and the children had found places for their boxes, Miss Finstock got out a huge sheet and spread it on the floor.

"This is our banner," she said. "We are going to hang it from the roof-top, so that everyone who goes past will see it."

"They will think we are airing the beds," said Zafar.

"We are going to write on it," said Miss Finstock, and she frowned at Zafar because she thought he was being cheeky. She took a crayon and drew huge letters on the sheet. "Do you know what this is, Duncan?"

"A snake," said Duncan, and hid behind Robert.

"Silly little boy," said Tracey. "It's an S. What will the words be, miss?"

"The banner says SAVE OUR SCHOOL," said Miss Finstock. "Now I want you to colour in the letters so they are very clear and bright. We will use paint and you must be very careful.

One letter each. Twins, you can just help me stir the paints, because you might go over the edges of the letters."

Janet painted the S in red, then she helped Zafar to finish another S in green. One of the twins spilt some brown paint on the banner, but it was only on the very corner. Two of the grown-ups carried the banner carefully out into the playground, to hang it from the chimneys as soon as the sun had dried the paint.

Miss Finstock stretched. "I'm stiff after bending down for so long," she said. "We'll have a gallop round the grass to stretch our legs."

As they were galloping, two men in white jackets and trousers came into the playground carrying something very heavy between them. The children ran to see what it was. It was an enormous iced cake with pink children iced all round the edge. In the middle it said SAVE OUR SCHOOL.

The men in white jackets could hardly speak English. Miss Finstock talked to them. She told the children that the men worked at the bakery

with Zafar's big sister, and the cake was a present from all the bakery workers.

"It's really huge," said Vernon. "Just think of all the bakers helping to make it for us."

"It's not only from the bakers," said Miss Finstock. "It's from the sweepers-up, and the bakery van-drivers, and the people in the office who take orders for bread and cakes. Some of them have children of their own, and they all believe the school should be kept open."

Mrs. Cowley fetched a long knife and they cut the cake. Janet was sad to see it cut up, but it was delicious. The bakery men watched them eat it. Janet was careful to look very pleased, because the men would understand looks even if they did not understand what she said.

4   A Knock in the Night

Visitors came to the school all day. Reporters and photographers came from two different newspapers to find out how the school was being saved, and to take pictures. Then a van parked outside the gate and some people climbed out of the back with a big television camera. Mrs. Cowley said they could bring the camera into the playground if they would show the children how it worked.

All the children had a look through the camera viewfinder, and Janet tried talking into the microphone. The television crew took some film of the children dancing the square dance that they had been practising all term.

"Watch the news this evening," they said.

"You might see someone you know." Then they took the camera back to the van and drove away.

Vernon's dad brought the children's dinner. Patrick's father had helped Bernie and some of the other little children to make jelly for everyone to have after it, and then there were oranges that one of the newspaper reporters had brought as a present.

While everyone else was playing outside, Tracey's twins went indoors. They got out all the puzzles and mixed up the pieces. Zafar and Janet spent most of the afternoon sorting them out again and putting them together.

Patrick's dad read the story of the Sleeping Beauty. Janet listened because she liked the story, but at the same time she could not stop thinking about the changes at school. It felt busier and more excited than usual. Janet felt excited too. It felt more like the children's own school now, as though it belonged to them, instead of belonging to grown-ups who allowed the children to come there each day, and told them what to do.

When Patrick's father read about the princess falling asleep, everyone was very quiet. He read about the plants growing up around the

enchanted palace while the guards snored on the palace steps. Janet looked at all the children sitting close together and very still, and suddenly she felt very angry that the Council should think of spoiling it all.

Later, Tracey's mum brought in her portable television and they all watched the news. At last the news reader shuffled her papers and announced, "Yesterday afternoon a school due for closure was occupied by the children and

their parents. Sarah Accleton visited them today."

Then they saw their own school on the television screen. First the playground with the murals that the big children had just painted on the wall, then they saw the children, themselves, doing their square dance. Janet saw herself dancing. She knew it was herself because of her stripy jumper and dungarees, but it was a strange person and its feet were too big for dancing.

"I look silly," said Janet. "I should have hidden. They shouldn't show people on television who are not beautiful."

"You are beautiful," said her dad. "You all looked nice on the television. I think people who saw the news will want the school to stay open. Maybe they will come and help us."

"Everyone in the town is interested," said Tracey's dad, who had just got back from the car factory. "All the people I spoke to at the factory today were saying what a disgrace it is to shut the school. Those Councillors never thought that so many people would care. We'll show them how many people care, and I reckon they'll have to change their minds."

"Did you see me on the telly, Dad?" asked Tracey. "I was on it, too, and I put my tongue out, did you see?"

"That is very silly," said Zafar. "You should never dance with your tongue out. You might

trip and bite it off. You could swallow it."

"You had better get your wendy house sorted out, Janet," said her dad. "It's just about bed time. Zafar's going home in a minute. The grown-ups will be talking for a while, but that won't bother you, will it?"

"What are you going to talk about?" asked Janet.

"We have to make a list of who is to bring the children's dinners in each day, and we have to make a few rules to keep the school tidy. Visitors must clear up their blankets in the morning so there is room for you to play in the hall, and children must not touch the typewriter. Did you see what Bernie did with it this morning? It was all jammed up and the ribbon was in knots."

"Will you make a rule about cigarettes?" said Janet. "Grown-ups should not smoke in our classrooms."

"That's true," said her dad. "I'll suggest that. The other thing is the Council meeting tomorrow. The Councillors will be meeting in the morning. We need to persuade them to change their minds. Tonight we'll work out the best way to make them take notice of us."

Janet listened to the grown-ups talking as she lay in the little bed with the curtains drawn shut. At last she heard them agree that nobody should smoke cigarettes in the classrooms. Vernon's dad grumbled a little and went out into the playground to finish his cigarette. Janet fell asleep.

She slept for a hundred years. At least, it seemed like a hundred years. While she slept, creepers grew all over the doors and windows and the playground grew full of bushes and trees. The Council had shut the school and all the children were asleep at their desks.

Janet was still waiting in her dream for someone to break the spell and save the school, when flashing lights woke her. They were flashing through the classroom windows and shining off the ceiling and walls. Then there was a knock on the door. Janet was frightened. It was so dark except for the flashes of light, and so quiet except for the knocking. No-one else seemed to have heard.

She drew the wendy house curtains. The patches of light moved unsteadily across the room. First the clock was lit up, then the project

that Zafar had pinned up. Then it went dark, and the banging started again.

"Dad!" whispered Janet. "Who is that at the door?"

Her dad never woke up quickly. "What?" he said from inside his blanket. "Get the breakfast yourself. Make some toast. I'm asleep."

The light came flashing round again. This time it stopped for a second on the blackboard and lit up Miss Finstock's message about P.E. shorts.

"No," said Janet. "Not breakfast. It's the middle of the night. I think the Council are here."

Her dad sat up quickly, still wrapped in his blanket like a long caterpillar. He called to Tracey's mum who was sleeping by the door.

"I'm not opening the door," she said. "It's probably the Council." She unwound her blanket and stood on the table, to talk through the top window. The knocking stopped and the light stayed outside. Janet could not hear what was said. She saw the grown-ups sleepily sit up all over the classroom, a whole field of giant caterpillars. Then the people outside went away. Janet heard the click as they shut the playground gate. The caterpillars lay down again.

"It's all right," said Tracey's mum. "That

was the police. The school happens to be on their beat, and they were just checking up."

"Are the police trying to shut the school, as well as the Council?" asked Janet.

"The Council may well ask the police to help them," said Tracey's mum. "But these policemen were quite friendly."

"If they were friendly," said Janet, "why did they wake us up in the middle of the night, and frighten us?"

"Don't be frightened," said her dad. "We're quite safe in here. If the Council will just agree that the school is too useful to close down, then we can stop sleeping here at night, and the police can stop worrying about what is going on here. You get back to sleep, Jan."

5 Marching into Town

In the morning, Nicole's mother came to school with her box of make-up. First she painted Nicole's face and made her look like a clown.

"This is for the carnival procession," she said. "Shall I paint you next, Zafar?"

"Yes please," said Zafar. "I want to be a tiger. You say my name funny, don't you? It's Zafar – Za-far."

"That's because I'm French," said Nicole's mother. "I say a lot of things funny. But as long as you can see what I mean, we shall be all right. We will put yellow on your cheeks first, and I think blue whiskers will suit you well."

Janet had never seen so many tubes and jars of different colours as Nicole's mother had in

her make-up box.

"Can I be a purple clown?" she asked. "This dark purple for my face, and a sad white mouth."

Nicole's mother painted all the children. Then they got out the dressing up clothes. There were not enough to go round, so Janet wore her dad's T-shirt. It was much too big, which looked right for a clown. But her dad did not like having his jumper next to his skin. He said it was itchy and it made him jump up and down and flap his arms. Janet liked it when he was in a mood for fooling around. At home he was sometimes grumpy, but a crowd of people put him in a good temper.

"What is the carnival procession for?"

Janet asked her dad.

"We want everyone in the town to notice us," he said. "The more fun it looks, the more people will come with us. If there is a really big crowd to meet the Councillors, they will have to take notice of us."

"Where are we going to meet them?" asked Janet.

"At the County Hall," said her dad. "That is where they have their meetings. We will speak to them as they go in, and ask them to let the school stay open."

Some people had to stay and guard the school. The rest marched out into the town in a long procession. At the front was a lorry with a band on it. There were clowns playing guitars and a trumpet and a violin. The lorry was decorated with balloons and coloured streamers.

Then came the school children. Some of the younger brothers and sisters were in prams and push-chairs. Zafar's mother had a notice on her pram saying KEEP THE SCHOOL OPEN FOR ME. Patrick and Bernie had paper flags which said SAVE OUR SCHOOL.

Tracey's father came. He had brought a lot of his friends from the car factory. They had decided not to go to work, because it was more important to tell the Council what they thought about the school. Some of the bakers joined the procession, and some firemen wearing their uniforms. There were two clowns who walked along the pavement giving out pieces of paper to anyone who was passing by. The papers explained why they were all marching down to meet the Council.

Shoppers stopped to watch as they all walked through the town. More people joined in with the procession. When they came to the centre

of town, the procession stopped and everyone crowded into the square.

"That's the County Hall over there," said Janet's dad. "Those people going in now are the Councillors. They are the ones who decide whether schools shut down or stay open, and how much money is spent on teachers and books."

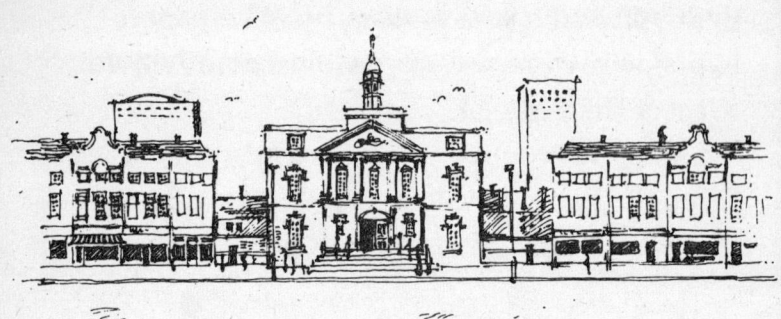

One of the Councillors stopped before she went in. "Here's a Councillor who wants the school to stay open!" Patrick's mother shouted, and everyone cheered.

"I've been against the closure all along," said the Councillor. "Your campaign has made quite an impression. We may win the vote today, if we can get it on the agenda."

"What did she say?" asked Janet.

"The Council may change their minds," said her dad.

Another Councillor went into the building. He did not want to speak to anyone from the carnival procession. He stepped right over one of the twins as though it was only a little patch of mud. Then he stopped on the huge doorstep and turned round. "This whole matter has been through committee," he said,

"and been ratified by full Council. Your efforts to stir up opposition, and your use of these babes in arms as hostages, are a disgrace. The issue should not be reopened. I shall oppose it all the way." Then he went in.

"He was horrible," said Janet. "What did he say?"

"The Council won't change its mind," said

her dad, "if he has his way."

"What about the babies' arms?" asked Janet.

"That means you," said her dad. "That man thinks you are too small to worry about whether the school stays open or shut. I don't like you to worry about it either, but it's the Council's fault that we are worrying at all, isn't it?"

Janet did not like being called a baby. She went and watched Patrick's little sister Bernie doing some very brave things on the stone wall round the County Hall.

Vernon was watching too. "I think tight-rope walking is easier if you are small," he told Janet. "Bernie's head is close to her feet. My head is so far up in the air that it waves around in the breeze and gets dizzy. Look what she's doing now."

"I never was an acrobat even when I was as small as Bernie," said Janet. "It must be her special talent."

"My special talent is cooking," said Vernon. "I know a lot about food."

"You take after your father," said Janet. "I take after mine. My dad and me, we don't have special talents."

"It's time for the meeting to start now," said Janet's dad. "Tracey's mum has gone in to watch. She will come out and tell us as soon as there is any news."

Janet hopped up and down. "They can't take long to make up their minds, can they?" she said. "Now they know that all these children want to stay at the school, and all the factory workers care about it enough to miss work. The Council must know that they can't shut the school when the whole town wants it to stay open."

"I don't know how long they will be," said her dad. "It's horrible waiting, isn't it? I feel fidgety, too. I'll run and get something for us to munch while we wait."

He ran off on his long fidgety legs. Janet went to stand by the great wooden doors where the Councillors had gone in. Suddenly the door opened, and Tracey's mum rushed out.

"We've won!" she said. "They took the vote again, and the school stays open! And not only that, but they are going to take on another teacher so that the second classroom can be used as well!"

Janet looked at Tracey's mum. She had never seen a grown-up so excited. Patrick's mother looked just the same, pink and happy. Vernon's father had a huge smile inside his beard, and he threw away his cigarette and picked up the nearest child to give him a big hug. The nearest

child was Zafar, who wriggled down to the ground again.

"Well, that's a nice surprise," said Mrs. Cowley. "We can enjoy the holidays now. I thought I would be spending them looking out for a new job."

"I thought we would spend the holidays

camping at school," said Zafar. "But we won't need to guard it any more, now they are not trying to close it down. I've missed my chance of sleeping in the wendy house. But I am glad we have won."

Janet went to look for her dad. When she saw him, she found that she could not tell him the good news because her eyes and nose were full of tears.

"What happened, Jan?" asked her dad. "Did you fall off the wall?"

Janet shook her head and wiped her nose on her dad's shoulder.

"Your clown's face is getting smudged," said her dad. "We won, didn't we? I knew we would! I knew they would change their minds when they saw we cared, and we wouldn't give up the school. You can see I thought we would win. Look how many cakes I bought, to celebrate."

"Dad!" said Janet. "All those cakes! That must be all your pub money gone!"

"We don't often have a great victory like this to celebrate, do we?" said her dad. "Just for once I'll stop in on Friday night and recover from all this excitement."

"Janet," said Vernon. "Your dad has a talent for knowing just when people most need to eat. Perhaps you will take after him."

"I shall be a Councillor," said Janet. "With a talent for knowing all the things that people most need. I shall make sure that children can go to schools near their own homes, and that the teachers have money for yellow paint when they need it. And when people come to talk to me, I shall not call them babies, or say they are a disgrace."

They walked home, full of cake and very happy. When they reached Harwell Road, Vernon and his father turned off. They waved to Janet, and she shouted at the top of her voice, so that the whole town could hear, "See you next term!"